Great Explorers

Christopher Columbus

by Jim Ollhoff

Visit us at www.abdopublishing.com

Published by ABDO Publishing Company, 8000 West 78th Street, Suite 310, Edina, MN 55439. Copyright ©2014 by Abdo Consulting Group, Inc. International copyrights reserved in all countries. No part of this book may be reproduced in any form without written permission from the publisher. ABDO & Daughters™ is a trademark and logo of ABDO Publishing Company.

Printed in the United States of America, North Mankato, Minnesota
052013
092013

Editor: John Hamilton
Graphic Design: Sue Hamilton
Cover Design: Neil Klinepier
Cover Photo: AP
Interior Photos & Illustrations: AP-pgs 24 & 25; Corbis-pgs 6-7, 19 & 23; Getty-pgs 5, 9, 10-11, 15, 16, 17, 20, 21 & 29; Glow Images-pgs 14 & 18; iStockphoto-compass illustration; Mariners' Museum-pg 8; National Museum of Art, Architecture & Design-Oslo, Norway/artist Christian Krohg-pg 4; Thinkstock-pgs 22 & 27 & grunge map background illustration.

ABDO Booklinks
To learn more about Great Explorers, visit ABDO Publishing Company online. Web sites about Great Explorers are featured on our Book Links pages. These links are routinely monitored and updated to provide the most current information available. Web site: www.abdopublishing.com

Library of Congress Control Number: 2013931680

Cataloging-in-Publication Data

Ollhoff, Jim.
Christopher Columbus / Jim Ollhoff.
p. cm. -- (Great explorers)
ISBN 978-1-61783-964-1
1. Columbus, Christopher--Juvenile literature. 2. Explorers--America--Biography--Juvenile literature. 3. Explorers--Spain--Biography--Juvenile literature. 4. America--Discovery and exploration--Spanish--Juvenile literature. I. Title.
970.01/5/092--dc23
[B]   2013931680

Contents

The Risky Route to China

Below: Norse explorers, led by Leif Eriksson, were the first Europeans to discover America 500 years before Columbus.

Christopher Columbus was an Italian explorer who made four voyages for Spain across the Atlantic Ocean to the Americas. Some people think Columbus "discovered" America in 1492, but there were millions of Native Americans already living there. He wasn't even the first European to make the voyage. (Norse explorer Leif Eriksson landed in North America 500 years earlier.) Columbus didn't even accomplish his main mission, which was to find a fast trade route to Asia. But the voyages of Columbus opened the eyes of Europeans to the vast wealth and opportunity that was waiting in the Americas. The world would never be the same.

A monument to Christopher Columbus in Barcelona, Spain. Columbus's journeys in the late 15th and early 16th centuries opened the eyes of Europeans to the vast wealth and opportunity that was waiting in the Americas.

In the 1400s, the people of Western Europe wanted an easy way to travel to China. Merchants wanted to trade for Chinese silks, spices, and other exotic products. From the writings of Marco Polo, people knew the Chinese had better technology and a highly advanced economy.

Unfortunately, there was no safe route to China. Traveling overland was too dangerous. Bandits, tribal wars, and unrest made travel difficult. Traveling by ship was also very dangerous. A water voyage meant going south around Africa, and then continuing east. Storms, pirates, and leaky ships meant a very risky voyage.

People knew the Earth was round. Scholars estimated that the Earth was about 25,000 miles (40,234 km) around. People had known this since the time of Aristotle (384 BC–322 BC) in ancient Greece. Since they didn't yet know that North and South America existed, people believed that if they sailed westward across the Atlantic Ocean, they could get right to China. However, it would be a very long journey. They would not be able to carry enough food and drinking water on their ships to survive the incredibly long voyage to China.

That left the people of Western Europe frustrated. They wanted to get to China, but they didn't know how. Then, along came Christopher Columbus.

Explorers Ferdinand Magellan (with globe), Vasco de Gama (with emerald necklace), and Christopher Columbus (black hat) all sought to discover new lands and new routes around the world in the 1400s and 1500s.

Birth and Early Years

Below: When Christopher Columbus was 25 years old, the ship he sailed on was attacked and destroyed by pirates. Columbus floated on debris and swam back to the coast of Portugal.

Christopher Columbus was born October 31, 1451, although some historians argue about his exact birthday. He was probably born in the Republic of Genoa, in today's northwestern Italy. He was the oldest of five children. Columbus's father managed a tavern and was a wool weaver. Young Columbus helped his father in the family business. Genoa was a seaside town, so Columbus gained a lot of experience with ships. He loved the sea, and loved the adventure of being on the water. By his early teens, he was a regular sailor.

When Columbus was 25 years old, he sailed on a ship in the Atlantic Ocean off the coast of Portugal. Pirates attacked his ship, and it was destroyed. Columbus escaped. He used some of the ship's debris to help him float back to the coast of Portugal.

As a young man, Christopher Columbus loved the sea. By the time he was in his teens, he was a regular sailor.

In the 1400s, the Portuguese were good sailors who built great ships. Columbus liked it there. He made his home in Portugal, and from there sailed to far-off places such as Iceland, Great Britain, and Africa. Columbus became an excellent sailor. He was one of the best at dead reckoning, which is the ability to know where a ship is located based on its speed and direction. He understood ocean currents and knew how to manage a ship no matter what direction the wind was blowing. He had a knack for predicting storms based on clouds, temperature, and wind.

During this time, Columbus married a Portuguese woman named Filipa Moniz Perestrelo. The couple had one son, Diego, in about 1480.

Many historians believe that Filipa died soon after Diego was born. Columbus moved to Spain and met another woman, Beatriz Enriquez de Arana. They had a son, Fernando, in about 1488, although they never married.

Columbus read many books. He got to know the work of a geographer named Paolo dal Pozzo Toscanelli (1397–1482). Toscanelli believed—incorrectly—that the world was less than 20,000 miles (32,187 km) around. The ancient Greeks had correctly calculated that the world was about 25,000 miles (40,234 km) around. Toscanelli believed that traveling westward across the Atlantic Ocean was a fast way to get to China. Columbus accepted this idea, and became obsessed with traveling that route.

Planning The Voyage

King John II of Portugal

Columbus began to think constantly about going to China. He studied long and hard. He even had a copy of Marco Polo's book of travels in China. Columbus made many notes in the margins of the book. Columbus shared his idea with anyone who would listen. He needed help from others to pay for his voyage across the Atlantic Ocean.

Columbus went to the leader of Portugal, King John II, and asked him to fund a voyage. The king said no to Columbus's plan. However, after Columbus left, King John stole the idea and sent ships westward across the Atlantic Ocean. They didn't make it very far before they were driven back by storms.

Columbus explained his plans to King John II. The Portuguese king refused to fund Columbus's voyage, but sent his own ships. The king's expedition failed.

In 1485, Columbus next went to the royalty in Spain. Ferdinand and Isabella were the king and queen, and he finally got an audience with them. Isabella liked Columbus. However, Spain was fighting a war with the Moors, a collection of people across the Mediterranean Sea. Ferdinand and Isabella couldn't spare any money or ships. But Isabella, intrigued by the idea, gave Columbus money to stay close and promise to sail in the name of Spain.

Seven years went by. The Spanish were done fighting the war and ready to think about Columbus's idea. Spanish scholars said that Columbus was wrong about the size of the Earth. The scholars said that it was too far a trip to get to China. But Ferdinand and Isabella wanted to gamble. The Portuguese were going to Africa, and places farther and farther away. The Spanish royalty wanted to do something to get ahead of the Portuguese. Although Columbus's plan was risky, it was worth a try. They agreed to sponsor him. But then Columbus made some demands. He wanted his title to be "Admiral of the Seas," and he wanted to be the governor of all the lands he found. Plus, he wanted a percentage of any treasures he and his crew uncovered. Ferdinand and Isabella were outraged, but they finally agreed to his demands.

So, in 1492, King Ferdinand and Queen Isabella provided Columbus with a crew and three ships: the *Niña,* the *Pinta*, and the *Santa Maria*.

Christopher Columbus's first expedition included three ships: the *Niña*, the *Pinta*, and the *Santa Maria.* They departed from Spain on August 3, 1492.

First Voyage

Below: Rough seas pounded Columbus's ships as they made the long, treacherous journey across the Atlantic Ocean.

On August 3, 1492, Columbus set sail with 90 men. He was sailing into the unknown Atlantic Ocean. Some people thought he would encounter sea monsters, or pockets of ocean where the water boiled. No one knew what dangers lurked in that unexplored ocean.

Weeks became months. The sailors grew more and more scared that they would all starve to death. Columbus had figured out how to sail with the ocean currents. The currents would take them west, and Columbus knew how to use the currents to go back home. The sailors couldn't mutiny because Columbus was the only one who knew how to get home.

On October 12, 1492, Columbus reached land. The island was inhabited by friendly natives who welcomed the strangers and brought them food.

On October 11, they saw some vegetation in the water. This meant land was close. The next day they saw land—an island in the Caribbean Sea. They wept with joy and relief. The exact location of the first landing by Columbus is not known. Many historians think it was San Salvador Island, in the modern-day Bahamas.

Columbus expected to see the Chinese emperor and buildings of gold. But, he only saw Native Americans. He called them "Indians" because he thought he had landed in the islands near India. The Native Americans, possibly the Taino or Arawak Nations, were peaceful and friendly. They gave food to the sailors.

Columbus went on to explore the coast of Cuba, which he thought might be Japan. He explored Hispaniola (today's Dominican Republic and Haiti). He was exploring, but also looking for gold. He left a group of men on Hispaniola to start a settlement. Then, he headed back home. He hoped that the men he left behind would find a lot of gold.

Second Voyage

Columbus made it back to Spain in March 1493. He had forced some Indians to return with him, and he also brought back gold. Word of his discovery spread rapidly. He was a hero.

Within a few months, the Spanish put together 17 ships and 1,200–1,500 people. They wanted to start a colony. Rumors spread that gold was everywhere in the new lands, and many people wanted to go. In September 1493, the ships filled with colonists started out.

Right: In March 1493, Columbus returned to a hero's welcome in Spain. He presented gold and captive natives to King Ferdinand and Queen Isabella.

Left: Columbus's men threatened and enslaved more and more natives in their frantic search for gold.

When Columbus arrived in the Caribbean Sea, he was anxious to check on the colony that he had left behind on Hispaniola. He had ordered them to find more gold. He wanted to see if they were rich yet. When he landed, he found that all the men had been killed. The Spaniards had wanted to be constantly fed by the Indians, and they mistreated the Indian women. Finally, tensions rose and the Spaniards were killed.

Columbus's answer to the tension was to enslave more Indians. He forced them to mine for gold, even though there was little gold to be found. Unfortunately, slavery was common in Europe at this time. Columbus thought little of exploiting the Native Americans.

Columbus was still convinced that he had landed in Asia, and he continued to look for the Chinese homeland. His men began to express doubts that they were in Asia. Columbus threatened to cut off the tongue of any man who dared say they were not in Asia.

Most of the new colonists were disappointed in Columbus and disappointed at the lack of gold. They were unhappy with the living conditions. Most of them sailed back to Europe.

Third and Fourth Voyages

Opposite Page:
Queen Isabella
agrees to fund
Columbus's third
and fourth voyages.
Below: A map
showing the
routes of each
of Columbus's
voyages.

Revolts were brewing. People were threatening Columbus. Columbus was depressed that he couldn't find China. He returned to Europe in early 1496. He was no longer a hero.

He persuaded Queen Isabella to fund one more voyage. But this time, he had a hard time getting a crew. People had heard that there was no gold, that colonists got sick and died, and that Columbus was a rigid and ruthless leader. Finally, Queen Isabella offered freedom to criminals and prisoners if they would go with Columbus. So, in 1498, Columbus returned to the Americas for a third time, but with a crew of malcontents and criminals.

COLUMBUS'S FOUR VOYAGES

1. VOYAGE: 1492–1493
2. VOYAGE: 1493–1496
3. VOYAGE: 1498–1500
4. VOYAGE: 1502–1504

Above: A modern-day view of Venezuela. When Columbus explored this beautiful part of the South American coastline, he thought he had found the Garden of Eden.

This time, Columbus explored Venezuela, along the coast of South America. It was so beautiful that he thought he had found the Garden of Eden. He knew by the volume of fresh water flowing into the ocean from a river that he had landed on a continent instead of an island, but he still believed that China lay to the north.

Meanwhile, the settlers on Hispaniola were revolting. Columbus didn't know how to manage the lawlessness, so he ordered that many of the men be hanged.

In 1500, the Spanish sent an envoy, Francisco de Bobadilla, to investigate what was going on in Hispaniola. Bobadilla arrested Columbus and sent him back to Spain in chains.

When Columbus returned to Spain, Queen Isabella freed him. But Columbus still pushed for another mission. He thought China was just west of modern-day Florida.

In 1502, Queen Isabella reluctantly gave Columbus four ships for his fourth and final voyage. The ships were in poor condition, and they barely made the trip across the Atlantic Ocean. When he tried to visit Hispaniola, he was denied entrance. He read the weather patterns and knew a hurricane was coming.

Above: In 1500, Columbus returned from his third voyage in chains. Queen Isabella freed him. In 1502, she reluctantly provided the explorer with ships for a fourth voyage.

Francisco de Bobadilla, the person who had arrested him a few years earlier, was leaving with several ships to return to Europe. Columbus told him about the incoming hurricane, and begged him to wait. Bobadilla ignored Columbus and set sail for Europe. The hurricane struck, and Bobadilla and almost all his ships were lost.

Columbus went on to explore Central America, but his ships were rotting out beneath him. He tried to make it back to Hispaniola, but his ships broke up and he found himself stranded on the island of Jamaica.

Final Years

Columbus and his crew spent a year stranded on Jamaica. Finally, a rescue ship arrived from Hispaniola. Columbus sailed back to Europe as a passenger. He was in ill health. He had gout and temporary blindness. His body was wracked by arthritis, and he was depressed. He had hallucinations, and would sometimes fall unconscious. He felt that God had abandoned him and he was mystified that no one understood his accomplishments. Columbus was a defeated man.

Below: A modern-day replica of Columbus's *Santa Maria* sails near Portugal.

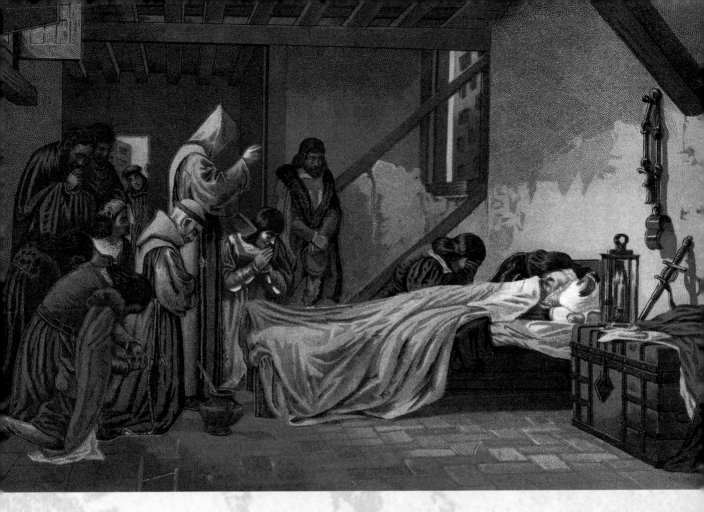

In November 1504, Queen Isabella died. She was Columbus's last supporter. Columbus did some writing, but his works were rambling and sometimes nonsensical.

On May 20, 1506, Columbus died in Valladolid, Spain, at the age of 54. He died probably still believing he had found Asia. His remains were moved several times. For many years two different places said they were the final resting place of Christopher Columbus: Santo Domingo in the Dominican Republic (Hispaniola) and the Cathedral of Seville, in Spain. In 2012, DNA testing showed that the remains in Seville were those of Christopher Columbus.

Above: Explorer Christopher Columbus died on May 20, 1506, in Valladolid, Spain, at the age of 54.

Columbus's Legacy

In real life, heroes are not always completely good. Villains are not always completely bad. Columbus was one of those people who are not easily put into a single category.

He was one of the best navigators ever to sail the seas. He could sense changes in the weather, he figured out ocean currents, and he always knew where in the ocean his ship was located. He was a great sailor, but he was a terrible governor. On land, he was a ruthless and barbaric leader who thought nothing of exploiting and enslaving other human beings.

Columbus was a man with a historic, world-changing vision. However, this vision kept him from seeing what was happening around him. The man with a world-changing foresight may have never realized that he had stumbled onto a new continent.

He was determined and headstrong. But he became arrogant, and didn't understand why others couldn't see his vision. His vision became an obsession. His obsession finally became madness.

Columbus opened the Americas for Western Europe. That changed the world forever. In some ways, it was good. In other ways, the change was terrible.

Right: Christopher Columbus was a visionary and a skilled sailor, but also a terrible governor and ruthless leader. He opened up the Americas, changing the world forever.

Native Americans were exploited and killed for hundreds of years. Within a few years of the discovery of the New World, the horrific African slave trade began. But Columbus didn't cause the exploiting and slavery all by himself. Columbus was a man with a single mission: he simply wanted to find a way to China.

One of the explorers who came after Columbus was Amerigo Vespucci. He lent his name to the new continent. Several cities in North America are named after Columbus, including the District of Columbia.

Columbus wasn't the first European on North American soil. Four hundred years earlier, the Vikings tried to colonize northern Canada, but they left after a few years. Columbus wasn't the first, but because of him, Europeans stayed in the Americas. For that, he will always be celebrated by some, and despised by others.

Timeline

1451, Oct. 31	Christopher Columbus is born, probably in Genoa Italy.
1476	A ship on which Columbus is sailing is attacked by pirates. Columbus survives by swimming to Portugal.
1492	King Ferdinand and Queen Isabella of Spain provide Columbus with a crew and three ships: the *Niña,* the *Pinta*, and the *Santa Maria*. Columbus begins his first voyage in August. They reach land in mid-October.
1493, March	Columbus returns from the New World with gold and native captives. He receives a hero's welcome.
1493, Sept.	Seventeen ships filled with colonists start out for the New World accompanying Columbus on his second voyage.
1496	Columbus returns to Europe. He is no longer a hero.
1498	Columbus takes his third voyage to the Americas. He explores Venezuela, South America.
1500	Francisco de Bobadilla arrests Columbus in Hispaniola and sends the explorer back to Spain in chains.
1502	Queen Isabella gives Columbus four ships for his fourth voyage. Columbus explores Central America.
1503	Columbus is stranded on the island of Jamaica.
1504	Columbus returns to Spain.
1506, May 20	Columbus dies in Valladolid, Spain.

Glossary

CARIBBEAN

The islands and area of the Caribbean Sea, roughly the area between Florida and South and Central America.

DEAD RECKONING

The ability to know where a ship is located, based on its speed and direction.

DNA

DNA is short for the scientific term Deoxyribonucleic Acid. In living things, DNA is the material inside the center of every cell that forms genes. This material is inherited from a person's or other living thing's parents. A person's DNA is unique to that person.

GARDEN OF EDEN

A beautiful place that some religions believe was created by God for the first man (Adam) and first woman (Eve) to live in peace and tranquility.

GOUT

A disease that usually attacks the feet and hands, causing swelling and significant pain.

HALLUCINATION

The experience of seeing something that does not exist outside the mind. A hallucination can be caused by a disorder of the nervous system or in response to drugs.

HISPANIOLA

A large island in the Caribbean Sea. Today it is split into two countries, Haiti and the Dominican Republic.

ISABELLA

Queen of Spain from 1474–1504. She was Columbus's best supporter, providing him with ships and crews for his journeys.

MOORS

A collection of people across the Mediterranean, most of whom were Muslim and many of whom lived in Spain.

MUTINY

When the crew of a ship disagrees with the captain and tries to forcibly take it over.

NAVIGATOR

The person in charge of plotting and directing the course of a ship.

NEW WORLD

The areas of North, Central, and South America, as well as islands near these land masses. The term was often used by European explorers.

PAOLO DAL POZZO TOSCANELLI

A geographer who lived from 1397–1482. He believed—incorrectly—that the world was less than 20,000 miles around.

PIRATES

Outlaw seamen who capture and raid ships at sea to seize their cargo and other valuables.

Index